Monsters of the Deep

© Aladdin Books Ltd 1997
© U.S. text 1997

Designed and produced by
Aladdin Books Ltd
28 Percy Street
London W1P 0LD

First published in
the United States in 1997 by
Copper Beech Books,
an imprint of
The Millbrook Press
2 Old New Milford Road
Brookfield, Connecticut 06804

Editor
Jim Pipe
Design
David West Children's Books
Designer
Flick Killerby
Picture Research
Brooks Krikler Research
Illustrator
Francis Phillipps

Printed in Belgium

Library of Congress Cataloging-in-Publication Data
Ross, Stewart.
Monsters of the deep / Stewart Ross ; illustrated by Francis
Phillipps.
p. cm. — (Fact or fiction)
Includes index.
Summary: Presents information about such creatures found in
the world's lakes and oceans as Great White sharks, the Loch
Ness Monster, giant squids, and poisonous jellyfish.
ISBN 0-7613-0548-3 (lib. bdg.). —
ISBN 0-7613-0595-5 (pbk.)
1. Dangerous aquatic animals—Juvenile literature.
2. Monsters—Juvenile literature. [1. Dangerous aquatic
animals. 2. Aquatic animals.] I. Phillipps, Francis.
II. Title. III. Series: Ross, Stewart. Fact or fiction.
QL100.R68 1997   97-10081
591.6'5'09162—dc21   CIP AC

FACT *or* FICTION:

Monsters of the Deep

Written by *Stewart Ross*
Illustrated by *Francis Phillipps*

COPPER BEECH BOOKS
BROOKFIELD, CONNECTICUT

CONTENTS

Introduction   5

PART ONE: TERRORS OF THE DEEP
The Unseen Terror   6
Thar She Blows!   8
Killer Whales?   10
Shark Attack   12

PART TWO: SLIPPERY DANGER
The Eight-legged Peril   14
Terrible Tentacles   16
Mystery Monsters   18
The Evil Serpent   20

PART THREE: WATERY WOMEN
The World of the Mermaid   22
Singing in the Wind   24

PART FOUR: LAKE MONSTERS
The Loch Ness Monster   26
Croc Shocker!   28
The Razor-toothed Piranha   30
Freshwater Fiends   32

PART FIVE: STORMY SEAS
White Death   34
The Power of the Sea Monk   36
The Stormbringers   38
Fishy Friends   40
The Holy Waters   42

PART SIX: WHAT NEXT?
The Hidden Depths   44

The Ten Real Monsters   46
A Monster Glossary   47
Index   48

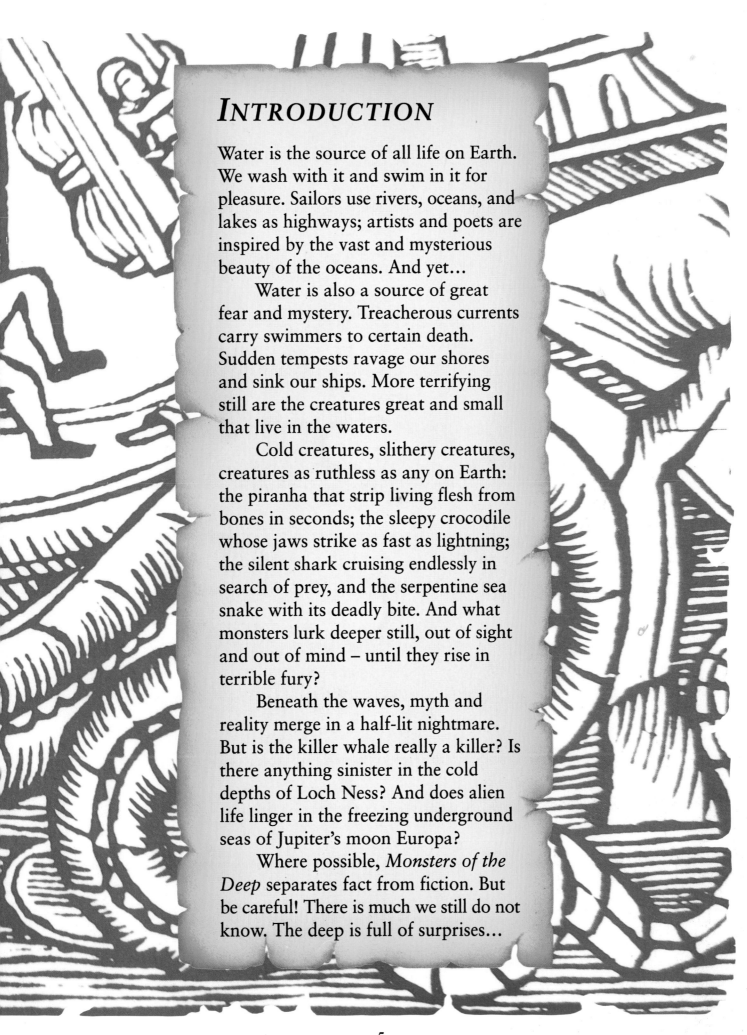

INTRODUCTION

Water is the source of all life on Earth. We wash with it and swim in it for pleasure. Sailors use rivers, oceans, and lakes as highways; artists and poets are inspired by the vast and mysterious beauty of the oceans. And yet...

Water is also a source of great fear and mystery. Treacherous currents carry swimmers to certain death. Sudden tempests ravage our shores and sink our ships. More terrifying still are the creatures great and small that live in the waters.

Cold creatures, slithery creatures, creatures as ruthless as any on Earth: the piranha that strip living flesh from bones in seconds; the sleepy crocodile whose jaws strike as fast as lightning; the silent shark cruising endlessly in search of prey, and the serpentine sea snake with its deadly bite. And what monsters lurk deeper still, out of sight and out of mind – until they rise in terrible fury?

Beneath the waves, myth and reality merge in a half-lit nightmare. But is the killer whale really a killer? Is there anything sinister in the cold depths of Loch Ness? And does alien life linger in the freezing underground seas of Jupiter's moon Europa?

Where possible, *Monsters of the Deep* separates fact from fiction. But be careful! There is much we still do not know. The deep is full of surprises...

THE UNSEEN TERROR

Over 70 percent of the Earth's surface is covered with water, and for all our modern technology, the oceans remain a harsh and unfriendly place for human beings. On land we are kings; on water we are vulnerable. The seas, rivers, and lakes are unpredictable, dangerous, and above all mysterious.

To explain the behavior of these great bodies of water, our ancestors invented water gods and goddesses. They also created a vast mythology based on half-understood water creatures. Many myths survive – and we are still adding to them! The movie *Jaws*, for example, turned the shark (*below right*) from a minor swimming hazard into a universal monster to be exterminated at any cost.

ALL IN THE MIND? Human imagination makes many sea creatures bigger and more dangerous than they really are. More people are killed each year by bees than sharks, for example.

The sea itself is the greatest killer, however, and ancient sea peoples recognized its danger. They believed that natural perils, such as drowning, storms, and whirlpools (*top*), had a supernatural explanation.

FRESHWATER THREAT

Strange creatures are not confined to saltwater. Early peoples across the world believed that beasts of all kinds dwelled in rivers and lakes. With real-life dangers like crocodiles nearby (*above*), you had a good look around before casting a net!

SALTY TALES. There are no stories quite like sailors' stories. And the more often they were told to a fascinated audience on the dockside, the stranger they became (*left*). Many mariners' fantasies – sirens, mermaids, and clashing rocks – became part of common folklore.

Monster Distortion
Up until the 19th century, glimpses of unknown but often harmless creatures, such as sea snakes, whales, and dugongs, gave rise to many imaginary monsters. Books and maps show fish and reptiles with huge heads and fangs, and long, writhing serpents (right).

FILM FANTASY. The depths of the seas and lakes are the last truly mysterious places on Earth. The movie industry has seized on this to populate them with a vast array of fantastic beasts – from the might of Godzilla to the razor-sharp teeth of Piranha!

Clash of the Titans
A classic sea monster appears in the 1981 movie Clash of the Titans (left), *bursting from the waves to terrify all but the brave hero Perseus. In Greek myth, Perseus rescues Andromeda using the head of Medusa the Gorgon to turn the monster into stone.*

DANGEROUS WHEN WET?
All past civilizations had special water gods and goddesses. In Greek myth, the sea god Poseidon patrolled the oceans in a shell-shaped chariot pulled by seahorses. More deadly was the goddess Sedna (*left*), whom the Inuits believed drowned sailors.

Many river names come from deities, such as the Don (goddess Danu) in Russia, the Thames (goddess Tämesa) in England, and the Orontes in Syria, after a hero who drowned (*right*).

THAR SHE BLOWS!

The sea was the Vikings' road to riches plundered from other lands. So they were eager to make their journeys as safe as possible. That meant building seaworthy ships, navigating carefully – and getting rid of dangerous obstructions, such as whales. They even called the seas the "whale's road." Harpooning a multi-ton monster from an open boat was difficult and extremely dangerous, however.

Though they didn't realize it, at that time hundreds of thousands of whales roamed the oceans. So the odd success provided meat for winter, but didn't make the "whale's road" any safer.

Watery Ghosts
Among the strangest whales are the ghostly beluga, or white whales (below). These intelligent creatures display a wide range of facial expressions – to human eyes they often seem to be smiling!

BIG DOWN UNDER

Whales are the largest creatures on Earth – *ever*. The biggest, the blue whale, can grow to 98 feet (30m) long and weigh 200 tons. But far from being sharp-toothed hunters, most of the great whales eat tiny shrimplike animals, called krill. They filter these from the sea using a system of plates called balleen (a growth a bit like human fingernails).

Until the 18th century they were thought to be fish, but whales are in fact warm-blooded mammals. They breathe through a "nostril" or "blowhole" on the top of their heads.

A WHALE OF A TALE. In 1851, American author Herman Melville (1819–1891) wrote the greatest whaling tale of all, Moby Dick (filmed in 1956, *right*). It tells of Captain Ahab's hunt for Moby Dick, a great white whale that has bitten off his leg. Ahab takes his ship, the *Pequod*, three quarters of the way around the world before he finds his prey. During the dramatic three-day battle that follows, Moby Dick kills Ahab and sinks the *Pequod*.

GIANT SLAUGHTER

Though whaling had been carried out by humans since the Vikings, by the 17th century it was a full-scale industry. The arrival of huge factory ships in 1925 began a forty-year period of mass slaughter, placing many species on the verge of extinction. By 1988, commercial whaling had stopped, but whales are still under threat from pollution and the overfishing of their food supplies.

WHAT A WHOPPER? The Bible's Old Testament tells how Jonah was thrown overboard from a ship (*left*) and saved from drowning when a whale swallowed him. After three days and nights in the beast's belly, Jonah was vomited up safely onto dry land. Pinocchio, the child carved from wood by a lonely carpenter, was also swallowed live by a whale.

Such stories may have some basis in reality. It was reported in 1863 that an American sailor named Peleg was swallowed by a huge sperm whale, and then vomited up again – unharmed!

KILLER WHALES?

Under the supervision of Herbert Ponting, the husky dogs were tethered on a large slab of floating ice. Suddenly the ice shuddered. Ponting looked around to see what was happening. Eight orcas had gathered beside them. Some had swum beneath the ice and were bumping it from below.

Ponting was terrified. He believed he knew exactly what was going on: The orcas were trying to get at the dogs by tipping them into the sea. Thanks to reports such as this, the orca got its undeserved reputation as the "killer whale."

PLAYFUL PIEBALDS

The beautiful black-and-white orca – also unfairly known as the killer whale – is a large, highly intelligent member of the dolphin family.

Playful, gentle, and inquisitive, they are famous for poking their noses out of the water to see what's going on. Perhaps this is what happened when the killer whales bumped the ice near Ponting. His tale even led to a U.S. Navy manual stating that orcas would "attack at every single opportunity" – completely untrue!

Beachcombers
For the orcas of the Patagonian coast of Argentina, seal pup is a great delicacy. They launch themselves right up onto the beach to grab a tender morsel (left), ignoring older seals and even a nosey camera crew in the water. There is no evidence of a so-called "killer" ever attacking a boat or a human being.

A Modern Myth

When Herbert Ponting, photographer on the British 1911 Antarctic Expedition, mistook orca inquisitiveness for aggression (main picture), *he helped create the myth of the creature's murderous nature.*

FREE WILLY? In the 1960s, scientists began to challenge the idea that orcas were man-eaters. When the beast's friendly nature was realized, some were put on display in ocean theme parks and taught tricks.

Further research showed that this unnatural behavior caused the creatures great stress. Though films like *Free Willy,* (1995, *left*) argued for their freedom, many orcas remain in captivity.

Narwhal

Unicorn

HORNY TUSK. The narwhal of the icy Arctic has long been regarded as an exotic creature. In the 10th century, the Vikings sold the narwhal's spiral tusk (actually a single tooth 9 feet long) to European merchants, pretending that it was a unicorn horn. England's Virgin Queen, Elizabeth I (1558–1603), kept a narwhal's tooth under her bed as she believed it had magic powers.

WHALE "SINGING"

Using modern acoustic technology, marine biologists have learned that several species of whales communicate with each other by means of low-frequency sounds ("singing") that carry many miles through the ocean.

Although we do not yet know what the different noises mean, they are further evidence of the creatures' sophisticated intelligence.

A Hard Tusk

The large tusks of the male walrus serve many functions – fighting other males, breaking holes in the ice, and as an ice pick to heave itself out of the water.

SHARK ATTACK

In January 1945, a fleet of B-29 Superfortresses took off from the Mariana Islands to bomb Japan. When their mission was over, most of the planes headed safely back to base. However, the crew of one badly-damaged machine had to abandon their aircraft and parachute into the Pacific Ocean. After several hours in the water, the dreaded fins were seen circling. Sharks! One crewman panicked and began splashing wildly to drive them away. Drawn by the noise, the creatures proceeded straight for him... Luckily, a rescue craft arrived shortly after and lifted all but one of the airmen to safety.

METAL MEALS

Of the 350 species of sharks, only 32 have ever been proved to have attacked humans. Sharks kill only about 35-40 people a year, compared with the millions of sharks killed by humans. Research has shown most sharks to be shy and intelligent, with individual personalities and an ability to learn fast.

Human beings are not a shark's favorite meal, though Tiger sharks (*below*) do nibble at anything they come across, including swimmers. Other objects found in their tough stomachs include lumps of coal, cushions, a crocodile head, and – so it is reported – even a suit of armor!

SUPER SENSES

Sharks have a wonderful array of senses for detecting food. Their eyesight and hearing are excellent. They can smell flesh or blood many hundreds of yards away, and they even have sensors in the nose that pick up electrical currents created by muscle movement.

Fatal Attraction
An airman unwisely attracts the attention of sharks by splashing (main picture). Sharks often leave their prey alone after a first bite, and almost no victims are "eaten." Most die from loss of blood or drowning.

Ugly Mug
The bad reputation of the hammerhead shark (right) stems more from its looks than its behavior. There are four species of this wide-eyed predator, but only one is known to attack humans.

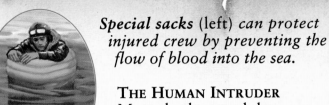

Special sacks (left) *can protect injured crew by preventing the flow of blood into the sea.*

THE HUMAN INTRUDER

Most sharks attack humans because they are testing if they are good to eat. But the gray reef shark attacks in defense of its territory. Before striking, it swims in a special way as a warning. If divers leave the area, as another shark would do, they will be left alone.

BATH BITERS. As well as being an entertaining movie, *Jaws* (1975, *above*) is also one of the most effective pieces of propaganda ever made. Before *Jaws*, most people saw sharks as a rare and occasional danger. After it, young children were even afraid to get into the bathtub before it had been checked for great whites! But the film did highlight how sharks often attack in shallow waters (*left*).

HARMLESS HORROR

Pytheas, the fourth-century B.C. Greek explorer who discovered that Britain was an island, was terrified of finding monsters in the unknown northern waters. The source of his fear was probably the huge but harmless basking shark (*right*), which eats only tiny plants and animals.

Basking shark

THE EIGHT-LEGGED PERIL

The diver fills his lungs with air and dives down beneath the surface of the warm tropical sea. A few powerful strokes take him to a rocky outcrop. He swims deeper, peering into shadowy crevices where he knows his prey is hiding. His body is crying out for air and he knows he cannot stay down much longer. Just when he is on the point of returning to the surface, a long, green-brown arm snakes out, grabs him around the leg, and drags him down...

This story is one of many depicting the octopus as an evil monster. But in real life, it is a timid creature, avoiding its enemies by swimming away or squirting ink.

The King of Hearts
The octopus gets its name from its eight legs ("octo" means eight). It ranges from the 26-foot (8-m) giant octopus to the small but deadly poisonous blue-ringed octopus (above). All have three hearts. When threatened, many varieties release a cloud of "ink" into the water around them and flee into the darkness.

GIANT GRIPPERS
Many are the tales of divers trapped on the seabed by the vicelike grip of the giant clam (*right*). Such a horrible fate is possible, for the largest clams weigh more than 550 pounds (250 kg), and a force of almost 2,000 pounds (900kg) is needed to open their shell.

But, contrary to popular myth, the clam shell does not snap shut like a jaw. It takes three or four minutes to close fully, so you would have to be either asleep or unconscious to get caught!

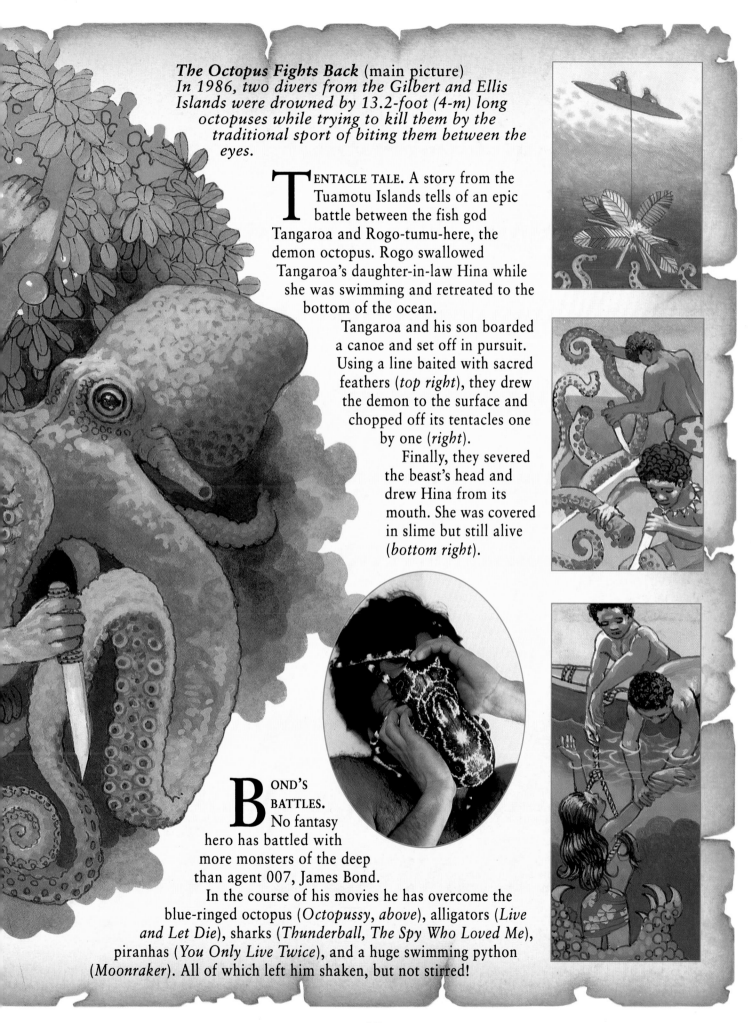

The Octopus Fights Back (main picture)
In 1986, two divers from the Gilbert and Ellis Islands were drowned by 13.2-foot (4-m) long octopuses while trying to kill them by the traditional sport of biting them between the eyes.

TENTACLE TALE. A story from the Tuamotu Islands tells of an epic battle between the fish god Tangaroa and Rogo-tumu-here, the demon octopus. Rogo swallowed Tangaroa's daughter-in-law Hina while she was swimming and retreated to the bottom of the ocean.

Tangaroa and his son boarded a canoe and set off in pursuit. Using a line baited with sacred feathers (*top right*), they drew the demon to the surface and chopped off its tentacles one by one (*right*).

Finally, they severed the beast's head and drew Hina from its mouth. She was covered in slime but still alive (*bottom right*).

BOND'S BATTLES. No fantasy hero has battled with more monsters of the deep than agent 007, James Bond.

In the course of his movies he has overcome the blue-ringed octopus (*Octopussy, above*), alligators (*Live and Let Die*), sharks (*Thunderball, The Spy Who Loved Me*), piranhas (*You Only Live Twice*), and a huge swimming python (*Moonraker*). All of which left him shaken, but not stirred!

TERRIBLE TENTACLES

Becalmed off the west coast of Africa, Dutch captain Jean-Magnus Dens orders his crew to clean the sides of the ship. A plank supported by ropes at each end is lowered over the side. Suddenly two vast arms rise from the sea and wrap themselves around the sailors. Screaming with horror, they are dragged off the plank and into the ocean. A third arm grasps a man on the rigging. Before he, too, is hauled into the sea, his colleagues hack off the monstrous arm with axes, and the giant squid slips silently back into the depths (*right*). Has the beast confused the ship with a whale, its natural enemy?

FISHERMAN'S FRIEND Some tales of the Norwegian Kraken (*top left*) speak of a giant squid (*above left*), others of a gigantic lobster. In one 18th-century story, Bishop Midaros celebrated Mass on one of these 1.25-mile-long monsters, believing it was a rock! As it gathered vast quantities of fish with its enormous tentacles, fishermen liked to have a Kraken around – as long as they were out of the way when it surfaced!

The Beast that Sucks
The most common squid is the harmless small creature that often ends up in a seafood salad (above). *Its giant cousin, which lives at depths of 9,600 feet (3,000m) or more, is rarely seen. A squid swims backward with "jet propulsion" by sucking in water with the folds in its body, then forcing it out again.*

Kanaloa, the Hawaiian devil and prince of the land of the dead, is an evil-smelling giant squid. He can adopt human form and lives on a magic island floating in the clouds.

LEGGY LEVIATHAN

The leviathan (*right*) is a sea monster from Hebrew mythology. Some legends tell of many heads, others of hundreds of serpent legs!

DEVILS OF THE DEEP. In *Twenty Thousand Leagues Under the Sea* (1869), written by Frenchman Jules Verne and filmed in 1954 (*below*), Captain Nemo's submarine *Nautilus* is attacked by giant octopuses, or "devilfish."

Cruising off the coast of America, the *Nautilus* suddenly stops. Nemo brings it to the surface and sends the crew to investigate. The monsters have jammed the propeller and are crawling over the deck. In the fight, the beasts drag one poor sailor to a watery grave.

Razor-toothed Tentacles
The tentacles of the giant squid, each covered on the underside with hundreds of tiny but razor-toothed suckers, may extend to an amazing 96 feet (30m)!

HIDDEN POWER
Several ancient European cultures, like the Celts and Cretans, used the squid as a symbol of the mighty powers that lie hidden beneath the surface of the sea (as on this Cretan weight, *left*).

17

MYSTERY MONSTERS

Most sea-monster stories arise out of a mixture of ignorance and exaggeration. One spring morning in 1925, for example, a group of people were taking a stroll along the shore in Santa Cruz, California. As they rounded a rocky outcrop, one of them stopped and pointed at something lying on the beach ahead of them. What on earth was it? Approaching carefully, they found themselves beside the partly decomposed corpse of a gigantic beast. It had a long, lean body and, weirdly, a huge head with a beaklike mouth. Since it looked like nothing they had ever seen before, they all jumped to the same conclusion – it was a sea monster!

Odd Fish
Some of the stranger species of sharks and whales may have fed sea monster mythology. Certainly, anyone catching a glimpse of a beaked whale, sawfish, goblin shark (above), or hammerhead shark for the first time could be forgiven for thinking they had seen a monster!

SHOW A LIGHT!
Another source of beast stories is the array of strange-looking creatures that are sometimes dredged up from the ocean floor (*above*). Because they live in virtual darkness, many of these "monsters" create their own light. The hideous hatchet fish uses luminous patches inside its mouth to guide smaller fish in.

There is a glowing red light below one eye of the rat trap fish, while the greedy gulper eel gets its victims' attention with a light on the end of its tail. The deep sea dragon has light cells running along its body.

Gulper eel

Deep sea dragon

Rotten Evidence

Walkers examine the remains of a rare beaked whale (main picture). Until scientists made a careful examination of the remains, the creature was considered a genuine beast from the deep.

STRANGE SIGHTINGS

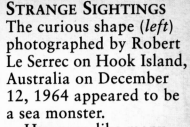

The curious shape (*left*) photographed by Robert Le Serrec on Hook Island, Australia on December 12, 1964 appeared to be a sea monster.

However, like many monster pictures only the eyewitness account confirms that it is genuine. A fraud could easily create a fake with a long piece of seaweed attached to a rock.

The Cornish Kraken

In recent years, there have been several sightings, both from ships and the shore, of the sea monster "mowgwyr" (literally, sea giant) in Cornwall, England.

In 1976, photographs were taken of it, showing a creature with a large body and a long, thin neck (above). Fantasy, hoax – or fact?

BIG MOUTH

Some monster sightings may be explained by "Megamouth." A survivor from the age of the dinosaurs, this 14.4-foot (4.5-m) long, 340-pound (750kg) shark was first discovered in 1976.

Like many of the largest creatures in the sea, however, it uses its huge mouth and tiny teeth to eat small creatures. Phew!

Yellow-bellied
sea snake

Banded
sea snake

THE EVIL SERPENT

March 23, 1830. The schooner *Eagle*, bound for
Charleston, South Carolina, was making good
time when the starboard lookout started shouting.
Captain Deland raised his telescope and scanned the
horizon. Yes, there was something strange out there.
He changed course toward what seemed to be an
enormous serpent, basking in the sun. Deland
ordered a man to shoot at it. The musket ball
struck the creature on the back, sending it
diving beneath the waves in a huge cloud
of spray. It then swam below the ship
and struck it several times with its tail
before disappearing. What was this
strange creature?

Rhinomuraena sea snake

Beaked Killers
*Sea snakes only grow
to 8 feet (2.5m), but
most are highly
poisonous. They pose
little threat to
humans, because they
remain far from the
shore. But the beaked
sea snake that lives in
the muddy shallows of
Southeast Asia kills
thousands of people
each year.*

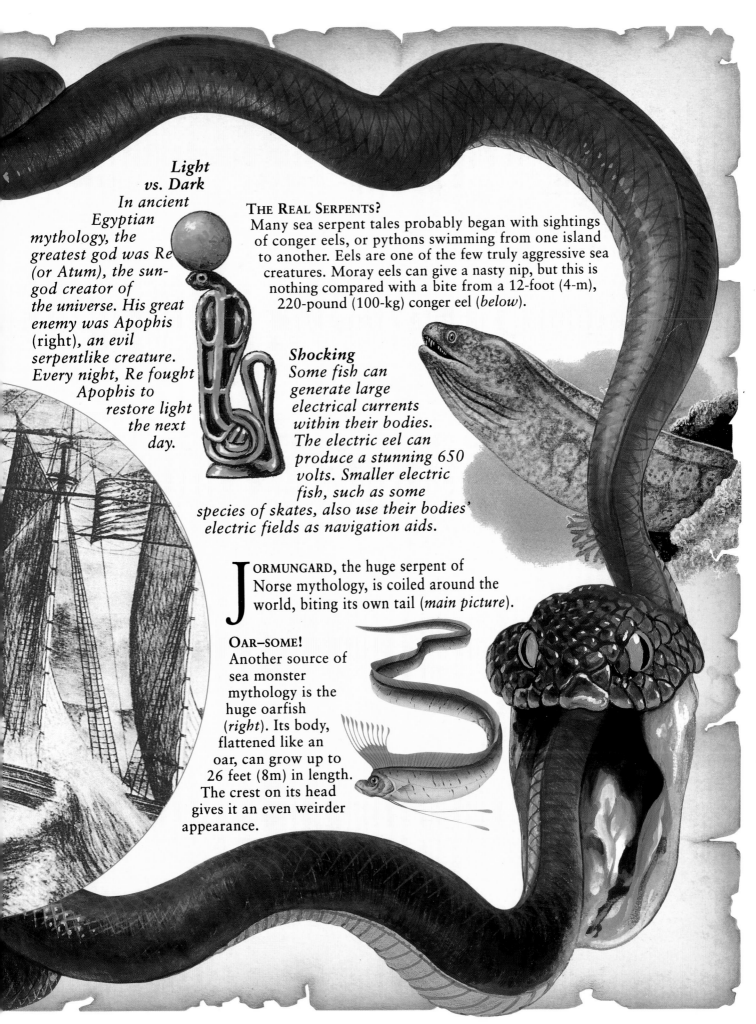

Light vs. Dark

In ancient Egyptian mythology, the greatest god was Re (or Atum), the sun-god creator of the universe. His great enemy was Apophis (right), an evil serpentlike creature. Every night, Re fought Apophis to restore light the next day.

THE REAL SERPENTS?

Many sea serpent tales probably began with sightings of conger eels, or pythons swimming from one island to another. Eels are one of the few truly aggressive sea creatures. Moray eels can give a nasty nip, but this is nothing compared with a bite from a 12-foot (4-m), 220-pound (100-kg) conger eel (*below*).

Shocking

Some fish can generate large electrical currents within their bodies. The electric eel can produce a stunning 650 volts. Smaller electric fish, such as some species of skates, also use their bodies' electric fields as navigation aids.

JORMUNGARD, the huge serpent of Norse mythology, is coiled around the world, biting its own tail (*main picture*).

OAR–SOME!

Another source of sea monster mythology is the huge oarfish (*right*). Its body, flattened like an oar, can grow up to 26 feet (8m) in length. The crest on its head gives it an even weirder appearance.

THE WORLD OF THE MERMAID

The explorer Henry Hudson (1550–1611) was as hard-nosed a sea captain as any afloat. This makes one entry in his log all the more surprising. At dawn, he wrote, lookout Thomas Hilles spied a young woman swimming near their ship. She had a full figure, white skin, and long black hair that spread out in the water behind her. She followed the ship until a wave broke over her and she disappeared. As she vanished, Hilles saw that instead of legs she had a long scaly tail like a porpoise. It was not a woman the man had seen, Hudson concluded, but a mermaid (*right*)!

The Real Mermaids
The most likely explanation for mermaid stories is the dugong. At a distance, a short-sighted sailor might think this gentle beast of the Indian Ocean and West Pacific was semi-human (above).

Other creatures that may explain merfolk myth include seals (left) and moustached walruses. In sunny weather, a creature's shape can also be distorted by the "mirage" effect of rising hot air.

INSTANT **DEATH.** A shrine on the Japanese island of Tango is dedicated to a local fisher boy Urashima, who married a sea maiden.

He went to live in her undersea palace, but after a time wished to see his parents again. The mermaid gave Urashima a magic box that would allow him to return home, as long as it remained closed. On finding he had been absent for hundreds of years, the boy opened the box and instantly shriveled into a skeleton (*left*).

Mer-Macho

The most common merperson in Muslim cultures is the so-called Sea-Turk (left). With his bare, muscular torso and rugged face, he is the very opposite of the seductive mermaid.

SOULESS MERFOLK

Most maritime cultures have tales of half-fish, half-human creatures. Babylonians worshiped the fish-tailed god Ea. Roman writer Pliny the Elder was sure merfolk existed. The medieval church believed in them too, but warned that they should be avoided as they lacked souls.

Fishing for Profit

The mermaid myth has always attracted tricksters. In 1826, an English priest wrapped his lower body in seal skins and sat on a rock singing "God Save the King" to his incredulous parishoners. In the mid-19th century, the American public was fooled with a monkey's body sewn onto a fish tail.

SCALY TALES. Although claimed sightings of mermaids are now rare, the creature is still a favorite in children's stories. In traditional tales, relations between merfolk and humans usually end in heartbreak. But in Disney's *The Little Mermaid* (1991, *above*) and the 1985 movie *Splash* (*below*) the mermaids live happily ever after!

SINGING IN THE WIND

The Greek hero Odysseus knew that no song was sweeter than that sung by the sirens to lure ships onto the rocks. He had to hear it. But no other member of his crew could be allowed to do so, lest they all be drawn to their doom. So he filled his sailors' ears with wax and had himself lashed to the mast. As the boat neared the island of the sirens, their singing became more and more alluring. Odysseus writhed with pleasure and screamed at his men to release him. But unable to hear either the cries of their captain or the seductive music, they rowed steadily on until the danger was past (*main picture*).

SEAMEN'S DELIGHT
The elaborately carved figures of scantily clad women that graced many wooden sailing ships were more than just decoration.
Sailors both yearned for female company and were also afraid of it, probably because they had so little interaction with women. As a result, women were felt to be unlucky onboard ship. But a female form on the prow was thought to have the power to calm storms (*left*).

Dragon Ships
The Vikings carved dragons on the front of their boats to scare the gods of their enemies (above). *The longship's red sail represented the dragon's wings, and the oars its legs.*

NAUTICAL NYMPHS
The ancient Greek sea-god Nereus had a hundred daughters, known as the Nereids (*right*). Dressed in flowing clothes, these beautiful water nymphs were carved on the sides of Roman tombs to suggest the soul passing from Earth to the spirit world.

The Sound of the Sirens
Odysseus is tormented by the singing of the sirens. On ancient Greek pottery (p.24, top) they were painted *as flying monsters. But in later folklore the flesh-eating sirens had fish tails, like mermaids* (main picture).

LADY OF THE LAKE. One of the best-known mermaids is the rather vague "Lady of the Lake" in the legends of King Arthur. In one story she rises from the lake to give and receive back the king's magical sword, Excalibur (*top*, from the movie *Excalibur*, 1981).

In another Celtic myth the Lady of the Lake buries alive the magician Merlin and rescues King Arthur from mortal danger.

Fishy Warning (right)
The folk of Caithness, Scotland, told of the Selkie, a seal people who became human when they took off their skin. If a human found it, they could marry the selkie.

STRAIT SAILING
In Homer's epic poem *The Odyssey*, Odysseus also meets the six-headed sea-monster Scylla (*above*). The beast may represent the treacherous straits of Messina between Sicily and Italy.

THE LOCH NESS MONSTER

In July 1933, Mr. and Mrs. Spicer were driving north along the narrow road that twists its way around the banks of Scotland's Loch Ness. As they approached a slight incline, a strange gray creature lumbered into view about 525 feet (160m) ahead of them.

Although its lower half was obscured by the hill, they estimated it was about 5 feet (1.5m) tall and 30 feet long. It had a long, wavy neck. As Mr. Spicer drove toward it, the monster crossed the road and disappeared into the undergrowth beside the loch. By the time he reached the spot and got out to look around, Nessie had vanished beneath the murky waters (*right*).

WHERE IS IT?

Nessie was first seen in 565 A.D., when St. Columba rescued a swimmer from its gaping jaws.

Since then hundreds of reports, some accompanied by fuzzy photos (*above* and *below right*), have come from the loch. In 1933, when Nessie-mania was at its height, a two-minute film was shot of a humped beast.

To try and settle the mystery of Nessie once and for all, in 1962 the Loch Ness Phenomena Investigation Bureau was set up. It collected all available evidence and organized scientific research. Since then, the loch has been patrolled by miniature submarines (*above*). But of the elusive Nessie – not a sign!

A LIVING DINOSAUR

One of the most common explanations of water monsters – including that of Loch Ness – is that they are plesiosaurs, aquatic reptiles thought to have died out 60 million years ago. The theory gained credence in 1938 when a living coelacanth, also believed extinct for a similar period, was found in the deep ocean. Other real monsters of the dinosaur era included the dolphinlike ichthyosaurs (*below*) and a sea crocodile known as the metriorhynchus.

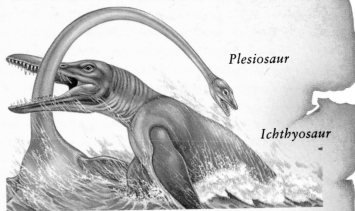

Plesiosaur

Ichthyosaur

The Ogopogo (below). *The monster of Lake Okanagan in British Columbia closely resembles Nessie, suggesting that a "monster belt" runs across the Northern Hemisphere!*

CHICKEN FEED. The aboriginal peoples of North America were convinced of the existence of lake monsters.

For example, the Shushwaps who lived beside Lake Okanagan placated their local beast – Naitaka (*right*) – by throwing a chicken into the lake before going fishing.

BOILED BEAST

The Native Americans of Puget Sound had good reason to be grateful to their super-god, Kwatee.

One day the ferocious monster that dwelled in Lake Quinault swallowed Kwatee's brother. The god immediately threw hot boulders into the lake, which boiled. The monster was cooked to death and Kwatee's brother was rescued from the creature's stomach.

CROC SHOCKER!

Ay the laundryman took his wash down to the banks of the Nile at dawn. He placed his basket on the ground, took out a robe, and dipped it into the river. On the other side of the river, a large green shape glided noiselessly into the water. It swam swiftly across the current, then stopped by a clump of reeds close to Ay. With only its eyes and nostrils above the water, it was all but invisible.

Ay came a little bit closer. Suddenly, the crocodile exploded from the water, its tail launching it 32 feet (10m) up the bank. Huge jaws closed around Ay's middle, and he hardly had time to scream. The beast shook him violently, then disappeared beneath the surface, still clasping its prey.

Croc-ville
The ancient Egyptians had such respect for the crocodile (above) that they gave the water god Sobek a crocodile head. In the oasis city of Crocodilopolis, sacred crocodiles were adorned with jewels and kept in luxury in large pools.

GRUESOME GRABBERS
Once it has grasped its prey in its 66-tooth jaw, the crocodile drowns it by dragging it under the water. It then breaks it into bite-sized chunks by literally shaking it to pieces. Not surprisingly, human victims often die of shock!

Though far more people are killed by snakes and insects than crocodiles, it is the gruesome nature of the attacks that makes the crocodile so feared and hated.

OLD CROCS
Sharp-eyed crocodiles and alligators, more intelligent relatives of the extinct dinosaurs, have been around for some 200 million years. The alligator is the more docile of the two and is distinguished by having no teeth visible when it closes its jaws. The Indo-Pacific crocodile, the largest of 21 different species, can measure over 23 feet (7m) from nose to tail.

Crocodile

Alligator

Clothes Hangers?
In Gambia, West Africa, crocodiles were looked upon as sacred. People kept them well-fed with fish, so they would be less likely to attack humans. Some brave folk even dried their clothes on the crocodiles' backs as they basked in the sun!

Ticking terror. The best-known crocodile in children's fiction is one that pursues the one-handed Captain Hook in *Peter Pan*, by J.M. Barrie (1860–1937). But whenever the beast closes on its pirate prey, Hook is warned by the clock ticking in the crocodile's stomach. In the movie *Hook*, when Peter Pan returns to Never Never Land, he finds the crocodile has been stuffed (*top*).

Public enemy no.1. In parts of Australia the crocodile was given legal protection in 1971. But occasional attacks on people and the hatred generated by the movie *Crocodile Dundee* (1986, *left*) have led to widespread and unnecessary slaughter.
   Although in Africa over 1,000 people are killed every year by crocodiles, in Australia less than one a year dies this way.

The Pull of Evolution
Writer Rudyard Kipling (1865–1936) used his knowledge of the crocodile's hunting techniques in How the Elephant Got Its Trunk: *A tug-of-war with a predatory croc results in the young elephant's nose being pulled into a trunk!*

THE RAZOR-TOOTHED PIRANHA

There was gold on the other side of the mountains, the Spanish conquistadors had been told. And they were going to find it – whatever the cost. They cut their way through thick forest, crossed rivers on makeshift rafts, and fought off attacks from the natives. Late one afternoon they came to a broad river. It had not rained for days and the main stream was reduced to a trickle between pools of standing water.

Without a second thought, the leading man began wading toward the opposite bank. After half-a-dozen strides he appeared to stumble. His face crumpled with terror and pain. "God help me!" he screamed. "The fish! I'm being eaten alive!"

The Red-bellied Biter
Of several species of South American piranha (above), only one, the red-bellied piranha (top), is a flesh eater that feeds in groups. Even so, it is dangerous to mammals only when herded together in shallow water. Its normal diet is fish, but sometimes it will go for animals that venture into the water. Attacks on people are very rare.

FEARSOME FISH
Far more dangerous than the piranha is the tiny candiru, which feeds on mucus and blood. It swims up streams of urine into the human body, where it cannot be extracted because of sharp barbs. Ouch!

Among big fish, the superfast barracuda, more feared than the shark in the South Pacific, also hunts in packs, while the pike (left) found in northern waters, hunts alone.

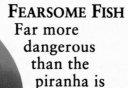

BONE-STRIPPERS. To thrill their audiences, the makers of monster movies usually exaggerate the danger of their subjects. This was certainly the case with *Piranha* (1978, *above*), in which mutant man-eating fish escape into the waterways, with bone-bleaching results!

THE AWESOME ANACONDA (*above*)
Large snakes are often shown attacking humans in films like the *Jungle Book* (1994, *below*) and *Anaconda* (1997), yet rarely do so. But 19.2-foot (6-m) pythons and 28.8-foot (9-m) anacondas have been known to eat leopards, deer, and crocodiles.

Slippery Stalkers
Swimmers beware, for deadly snakes also inhabit freshwater regions. Florida, for example, is famous for its water sports. But in the reeds lurks the cottonmouth moccasin snake, whose bite injects a wicked venom.

FRESHWATER FIENDS

The cuddly hippo wallowing in the mud or swimming along the river bed (*left*), seems a friendly enough animal. But the looks of this 8,880-pound (4,000kg) juggernaut are deceptive – the hippopotamus is thought to kill more people each year in Africa than the crocodile and lion combined. Its fierce tusks can reach 27 inches (70 cm) in length and its jaws are easily powerful enough to chomp through a small canoe (*main picture*).

If disturbed on land, the hippo charges toward the water along well-worn paths, trampling anything (and anyone!) in its way. It looks clumsy, but in short bursts it can run at 18mph (30kph).

OPEN WIDE!
Hippos live alone or in groups of up to two hundred. The herds are mainly females and calves, and a few bulls, which fight over the females. The bulls cannot find a mate without holding a territory, so they are very aggressive toward anything entering their patch (*right*). They can open their mouths incredibly wide (*above*) and do so when clashing with other bulls. In serious fights, they sink their teeth deep into their rival's back and shoulders.

Big Beaver
Even animals that present no threat to humans become fearsome beasts in mythology. In the tales of the Nez Percé people of Central America, the gentle beaver (left) *became the Wishpoosh, a giant monster who drowned any fisherman approaching its lake.*

DANGER TO SHIPPING

Some of the first Europeans to visit Africa reported seeing an elephant-sized water monster known as Mokele-Mbembe. The mythological vegetarian beast – part-hippo, part-rhino, part-crocodile – was said to sport a single horn, a long neck, and a strong serpentine tail, which it used to upset canoes.

THE BEAST OF THE NILE. The ancients knew the hippo as the "beast of the Nile." (Hippopotamus means water-horse in ancient Greek.)

The ancient Egyptians had several hippo gods and goddesses, including Great Mother Amenti ("she who brings forth the waters"), and Tawaret, a half-hippo, half-croc (*above*) who protects pregnant women. The hippo is also the most likely explanation for the Hebrew monster known as the Behemoth.

Lickin' Good

Perhaps because glands in its warty skin secrete poison, in Europe the ugly toad (right) *has long been linked with evil and magic. Crazy Californians even get a kick out of licking toads that secrete a dizzy drug!*

POISON FROGS

Several frog species also secrete poison, although many, including the 1.6-foot (0.5-m) diameter giant frog, are edible. The fluids from one small but colorful *Dendrobatus* frog can provide enough toxin to coat 50 of the deadly arrows used by the Amazon rainforest people.

WHITE DEATH

The first explorers of the polar regions encountered a new and merciless monster. It was a beast that crept up on them under the cover of darkness to clasp them in an iron grip from which there was no escape; that towered above them, taller than a cathedral; that crushed ships as if they were toys; that filled the air with terrifying howls and groans that sent shivers of terror down the spines of even the most hardened seamen; that wickedly hid its bulk beneath the sea, luring helmsmen into a false sense of security. And the name of the new sea monster? Ice.

HIDDEN MENACE

Icebergs (*top*) are formed when huge chunks of ice break from the end of a glacier (frozen river) and drift into the sea.

Before the days of radar they were a real danger to shipping, as the "unsinkable" *Titanic* discovered in 1912 (*below*).

Like the sea monsters of myth, the bulk of an iceberg is hidden beneath the water – only about one sixth appears above the surface (*above*).

Gripped by Icy Fingers (below left) *British captain John Franklin (1786-1847), a veteran of the Battle of Trafalgar, ventured into the Arctic in 1846 in a vain attempt to find the northwest passage from the Atlantic to the Pacific. His ship was held in the monstrous grip of pack ice in the Victoria Strait, and he perished the following summer.*

FINGERLESS FURY. No sea goddess is more terrible than Sedna, the monster of Inuit myth. Born of giant parents, the child would eat only flesh.

When she began devouring her sleeping mother and father, they decided to take her out to sea and dump her in the deep. Her father cut off her fingers one by one to stop her from clinging to the boat and she sank out of sight. The fingers became sea creatures and she now sits on the ocean floor, furious that she cannot comb her hair (*left*). She hates humans, and sends storms to drown them. The only way to please her is for shamans to comb her hair.

WHIRLPOOLS (*right*)

Whirlpools result from the meeting of swift ocean currents. They were a serious hazard to small wooden sailing vessels and, because of their mysterious power, the ancients believed they had supernatural causes.

The giant Charybdis made the huge whirlpool off the coast of Sicily by drinking and spitting out all the water of the ocean three times a day.

Small icebergs are called "growlers" because of the eerie sounds they make as they float. Combined with strange shapes in the ice it's no wonder that explorers imagined monsters!

THE POWER OF THE SEA MONK

To the people of coastal Japan and the Pacific islands the tsunami, or tidal wave, was a certain sign that terrible forces dwelled beneath the surface of the ocean. How else could they explain the giant walls of water that rolled across the sea and crashed into the shore with enough force to smash houses, uproot trees, and hurl fishing boats far inland? The mighty power behind the tsunami was the sea bonze, or monk (*left*), a weird-looking creature that not only stirred up storms and giant waves, but attacked unsuspecting boats as well. Whenever a sea bonze was felt to be in the vicinity, sailors did their best to keep him happy by performing a special dance in his honor (*main picture*).

CRUNCHING PLATES

An earthquake is caused by a collision of two or more of the enormous tectonic plates that make up the Earth's surface. When 'quakes occur on the ocean floor, they produce tsunamis (the Japanese word for "harbor waves"). The term "tidal wave" is wrong. Tsunamis (painted *below* by the Japanese artist Hokusai) have nothing to do with tides, which are caused by the gravitational pull of the sun and moon.

Curiosity?
In Polynesian myth, a tsunami occurred when a sea goddess arose from the ocean floor to come and see what humankind was up to.

36

DEVIL FISH
Various explanations have been put forward for the sea monk myth. The most likely is that he arose out of a distorted glimpse of the underside of a ray or skate. Seen from below, the mouth and gills of these queer-looking fish can look like a human face. The ghostly manta ray (*above*) was also known as the "Devil Fish" until scientists realized this gentle giant fed on tiny sea life.

Flood warning. In the Japanese version of the Noah myth, the hero Vaivaswata rescued a tiny fish and cared for it until it grew so big he had to release it into the ocean. In gratitude the fish warned him of a huge flood, then when it came, pulled him to safety (*above*) until the waters went down.

JELLY ALERT!
Poisonous jellyfish (*right*) kill far more people than sharks. The box jellyfish, which injects its victim with over 1,000 tiny needles, can cause death within five minutes. A jellyfish's venomous cocktail of toxins attacks either the heart or the central nervous system.

THE STORMBRINGERS

The storm season had already begun when the ship carrying St. Paul and his escort left Crete for Rome. Shortly after leaving port, a strong northeasterly wind blew up. After two weeks of bad weather, the captain found his ship lying off a sandy bay. It soon became caught in a current and ran aground.

According to the Bible, Paul told everyone – even the non-swimmers – to jump into the water. They would not be injured, he promised, because God was watching over them. Amazingly, all 276 passengers and crew came ashore unharmed.

A WATERY GRAVE
The sea itself is a greater killer than any creature in it. The ocean floor is often called "Davy Jones' locker," the resting place for the souls of drowned sailors.

Holy Protection (main picture)
In A.D. 61, St. Paul was shipwrecked on the coast of Malta. God's intervention, he claimed, saved everyone's lives. The threat of drowning is still very real. Even tropical waters are too cold for the human body to survive long in, and dangerous sea currents have the power to sweep you far out to sea.

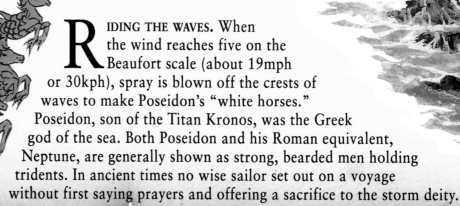

RIDING THE WAVES. When the wind reaches five on the Beaufort scale (about 19mph or 30kph), spray is blown off the crests of waves to make Poseidon's "white horses." Poseidon, son of the Titan Kronos, was the Greek god of the sea. Both Poseidon and his Roman equivalent, Neptune, are generally shown as strong, bearded men holding tridents. In ancient times no wise sailor set out on a voyage without first saying prayers and offering a sacrifice to the storm deity.

TO THE LIFEBOATS

Today, floods kill many thousands of people each year. In the ancient world, they could be catastrophic. Not surprisingly, most mythologies have a flood story. The best known is that of the Hebrew Noah (*right*), who saved living creatures by taking them with him into an ark when God sent a deluge to destroy the wicked world.

SORRY! The Hawaiian Noah was Praying Nu'u, who escaped the flood sent by the god Kane by building a huge boat with a house on top. When the flood had subsided, Nu'u sacrificed pigs and coconuts to Kane, who then slid down a rainbow to apologize for the destruction he had brought about.

Stormin' Sorcerers
People of pre-scientific times believed storms had a supernatural explanation.

As late as 1611, English playwright William Shakespeare gave the sorcerer Prospero "secret powers" to raise a great storm in his play The Tempest (left).

MOTHER OF ALL DRAGONS

According to Babylonian myth, Tiamat was a vast and terrible she-dragon (*right*). Before the sun god Marduk created the world, Tiamat was a great ocean of salt water.

When she refused to accept Marduk as her lord and master, he slew her and made the heavens and Earth out of her carcass. She lived on in folk tales as the devil, the mother of all dragons, and the source of all chaos, storm, and tempest.

FISHY FRIENDS

Sometimes a monster of the deep can be a human's best friend. One of the strangest tales of cooperation between animals and humans comes from New South Wales, Australia. Starting in 1830, each winter a pack of orcas, headed by "Old Tom," rounded up humpback and fin whales and drove them into shallow water.

Here the orcas attacked them until they lay exhausted on the surface and the whalers could kill them with harpoons (*right*). The corpses then sank to the bottom, where Old Tom and his pals chewed off the tasty tongues and lips. A few days later the bodies floated to the surface and the whalers towed them ashore for butchering. But after Old Tom's death in 1930 his pack never returned.

SMART SWIMMERS

Dolphins (*top*) and porpoises are toothed species of whales, famous for their high intelligence and agility. About 8 ft (2.5m) long, they can reach speeds of 35mph. The strangest-looking dolphin is the pink Amazon river dolphin (*left*). It is seen as a god by local peoples.

FLIPPERED FRIENDS. Because of their ability to learn tricks and their friendly ways, dolphins have always been liked by humans. There have also been several genuine reports of dolphins rescuing drowning swimmers, making them ideal heroes, as in the movie *Flipper* (*left*).

However, their ability to "speak" in a series of clicks and whistles may not be a language. It is probably more to do with finding and stunning small prey using sound waves in the water.

Cooperative Killers
Orcas hunt in packs of 4-40 animals known as "pods." They herd smaller prey into shallow waters by slapping their flippers on the water's surface and making whistling sounds underwater.

BLOW THAT HORN! Triton, the son of Poseidon and Amphitrite, was half-man, half-dolphin. The Greek poet Hesiod says it was Triton who blew a great conch shell to drive back the waters at the time of the Flood (*left*). Perhaps because he was half-dolphin, Triton was generally regarded as one of the more friendly undersea gods.

Music to the Ears
In Greek myth, the poet Arion was about to be thrown overboard by pirates when he begged them to let him play his lyre one last time. Hearing the sound, dolphins swam near the ship. Arion jumped into the sea, and they carried him safely to shore.

SEA SUCKERS
Horses have long been linked with the sea gods like Poseidon (*left*). True seahorses, however, are tiny, bony fish that suck small animals into their mouths through straw-shaped lips.

The male seahorse is unusual in that males give birth to the young rather than females (*right*). Sadly, these creatures are increasingly rare as they are used in Oriental medicine.

THE HOLY WATERS

Benia made sacrifices to the gods, climbed into his fragile canoe, and paddled out from the shore. Beyond the surf he waited, rattling coconut shells to attract the sharks' attention. Before long a huge shark swam up. Benia coaxed it closer and lowered a noose over the side. Then, cautiously slipping the loop over the creature's head, he pulled hard to tighten the knot. The shark went wild.

For two hours it thrashed furiously, trying to free itself from the rope and its attached float. Finally, when the beast was exhausted, Benia pulled its head from the water and slew it with his club. Killing the King of Fish made him one of the most respected young men in his village.

SHADOW SHARK
The shark is just one of many sea creatures regarded as holy. Some Pacific peoples will not eat its flesh, while others tell of sharks rescuing sailors from the sea. In Tahiti, the blue shark is said to be the shadow of the creator god Ta'oaoa. The divine Teanoi of the Gilbert Islands started life as a hammerhead (*above*). But when other fish plotted to kill him because he was so ugly, he fled to become a star.

Test of Strength
A young man from the Solomon Islands had to trap and kill the King of Fish to prove his courage and ingenuity (above).

Spirit Seekers
In the Solomon Islands gray reef sharks were thought to harbor the spirits of dead relatives, represented in rituals by shark masks (left).

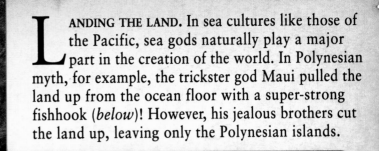

LANDING THE LAND. In sea cultures like those of the Pacific, sea gods naturally play a major part in the creation of the world. In Polynesian myth, for example, the trickster god Maui pulled the land up from the ocean floor with a super-strong fishhook (*below*)! However, his jealous brothers cut the land up, leaving only the Polynesian islands.

WATERY ORIGINS?

Some scientists believe that humans may have evolved directly from sea mammals – and some myths agree with this. In Micronesian myth, Latmikaik was queen of the oceans. In her watery bedroom she gave birth to shoals of fish (who built the land) and two sons. The beastly sons then mated with the fish to produce humans.

In Australian Aboriginal myth, fish (*above*) were created when the sun goddess Yhi melted the mountain ice into rivers.

BEASTLY TAXI The Hindu deity Varuna (*right*) is a kind of Hindu Neptune, or god of seas and rivers. In Hindu myth, he travels around his watery domain on the back of Makara, a beast that is part-crocodile, part-dolphin, and part-shark.

The Christian Fish
The Greek word ιχθυς (fish) is made up of the first letters of the Greek phrase "Jesus Christ, the Son of God, our Savior." Because of this, early Christians made the fish their symbol (above).

THE HIDDEN DEPTHS

We may well smile when we read of the mythological sea beasts and gods of earlier civilizations. But are we so different? We are just as frightened of unpredictable depths as our ancestors were. The sea still claims thousands of victims each year, and in books and on film we go on creating new stories about monsters that lurk beyond the range of our eyes. Tourists flock to Loch Ness in the hope of catching a glimpse of its monster.

When scientists announce that there are vast invisible seas beneath the surfaces of Mars or Jupiter's moons, we wonder what weird beasts may live there. For all our scientific advances, the deep has lost none of its mystery – and none of its terror.

MARINE MUTANTS
The awareness that we are gradually poisoning the planet has awakened out interest in the sea and all that lives therein. Each year tons of radioactive waste from nuclear plants are pumped into the sea. As well as killing off species, is it possible that we may be producing new ones that one day will rise to take a gruesome revenge on their creators?

Living Fossil (above right)
In 1938, the discovery of the coelacanth, thought to have been extinct for 400 million years, gave scientists hope that other prehistoric creatures have survived in the murky ocean depths. But would you want to meet one?

CAUGHT ON FILM?
A team of scientists are currently using a unique operator to track down the giant squid – a sperm whale. Why? Because they are the only creatures that know where the squids live (*left*)! Special cameras, nicknamed Crittercams (*right*), are strapped to the whales using biodegradable tape.

THE DEPTHS OF SPACE

Even science fiction writers are obsessed with the deep – perhaps space itself is just another uncharted sea? When our solar system is destroyed in Douglas Adams' bestselling book *Hitchhiker's Guide to the Galaxy*, the only creatures to be saved are dolphins. The recent discovery of subterranean seas on Europa, a moon of Jupiter (*right*), has led to fresh speculation that within them may dwell a whole new generation of monsters of the deep.

THE UNSOLVED MYSTERY. Since 1945, ships and aircraft have vanished in the Bermuda Triangle that lies between Florida, and the Sargasso Sea.

Electrical instruments fail there. The sea changes color. Violent storms are frequent. Are these caused by natural phenomena, such as undersea volcanoes? Or is there something more monstrous about that deadly patch of ocean?

A Nasty Attack of Crabs
The movie industry is the richest source of modern myth about monsters. Millions have followed the adventures of the gruesome Godzilla and Gorgo (above). Other movies show harmless creatures like crabs (right) transformed into hideous giants by nuclear pollution.

TEN REAL MONSTERS

1 The Sea (*left*)
The biggest killer of all is the sea itself. More people die from drowning each year than from attacks by sea creatures.

2 Great Great White
The ancestor of the Great White (*center page*) was enormous – about 46 feet (14m) in length. Its name, *Carcharodon megaladon*, means shark with big teeth – each tooth was larger than your hand. Luckily, this monster is now extinct!

3 Bull Shark
Carcharhinus leucas, the bull shark, is perhaps the most dangerous to humans. It swims far inland, and has been seen 830 miles (1,330 km) up the Zambezi River in Africa. Here it attacks unsuspecting victims in the murky shallows of lakes and rivers.

4 Sea Snakes
All sea snakes are poisonous, but *Hydrophis belcheri* has a venom a hundred times as toxic as the deadly Australian taipan snake. A bite can kill a human in minutes.

5 Blue-Ringed Octopus (*below left*)
The blue-ringed octopus, *Hapalochlaena masculosa,* contains a neurotoxin so dangerous that an antidote can rarely be used quickly enough to save the unlucky victim. The creature's bright colors tell other fish to stay well clear. But as it is so tiny this octopus can easily hide in something like a small glass bottle.

6 Piranha (*right*)
This fish is responsible for relatively few attacks on humans. But on September 19, 1981, more than 300 people were reportedly eaten by piranhas when an overloaded passenger boat capsized at the Brazilian port of Obidos.

7 Stonefish
This most poisonous fish is colored in a blotched pattern of browns and greens that blend in perfectly with the surroundings. It has a row of poisonous spines along its back that are strong enough to pierce a sandal. Its poison can kill humans by giving them a heart attack.

8 Puffer Fish
Some sea creatures are deadly even after they die. The puffer fish is a great delicacy in Japan, but its internal organs contain a strong toxin. Unlucky diners who have not had the dish prepared properly can die a very nasty death.

9 Australian Box Jellyfish
When approached by prey, the jellyfish releases a stinging thread which uncoils and turns inside out, exposing barbs. Some of the threads are hollow and contain a toxin which can cause death in humans within three minutes of contact.

10 Hippopotamus (*right*)
The hippo is one of the most dangerous of Africa's creatures. However, though bull hippos do attack boats that enter their patch of river, often these huge creatures trample people by accident as they take their regular route back to water.

MONSTER WORDS

Abyss Depths greater than 5,900 feet are known as the Abyssal zone. Here dwell strange deep sea fish such as the angler (*left*).

Cetacean The name for the group of mammals that includes whales, orcas, dolphins, and porpoises.

Deity A god or goddess.

Eels A type of long fish with few or no scales. In Ancient Rome, moray eels were kept as pets in large tanks. One Roman noble is said to have fed a slave to his eels as a warning to his other servants.

Electric fish Many fish have electrosensors that are sensitive to electricity in the water and can pick up the movement of other creatures. Some fish, such as electric rays (*bottom right*), have blocks of specialized muscles that produce powerful bursts of electricity.

Gills The breathing parts of a fish that do the same job as the lungs of a land animal. They extract oxygen dissolved in water.

Ink The device used by an octopus or squid to flee from an enemy. The ink turns the water black allowing the squid to make a quick getaway.

Kraken A Nordic myth that describes a squid- or lobsterlike monster that drags boats to the bottom. The Cornish Kraken is known as the "Mowgwyr."

Mermaid A creature from legend that is a woman from the waist up and a fish from the waist down.

Nymph A female deity that lives in mountains, rivers, and trees.

Orca The scientific name for a killer whale, *Orca orcinus*. In fact, orcas are more closely related to dolphins than to whales.

Reptiles Scaly, backboned animals that today live on land. However, in prehistoric times reptiles also lived in the sea, such as the plesiosaur, ichthyosaur, and tylosaurus (*above right*).

Sea cow A relative of the elephant that lives in shallow mangroves. It is known as a dugong in Asia and as a manatee in the Americas (*left*). It could be the basis for the legends of mermaids.

Serpent A snake.

Shaman A doctor-priest from North America or the Far East who works using magic and sorcery.

Shark A type of meat-eating fish that has a skeleton made of cartilage rather than bone. Most sharks must swim constantly to force water over their gills to breathe.

Tentacle A slender and flexible part of an animal used for feeling and grabbing, for example on the giant squid (*bottom left*).

Toxin A poison.

Tsunami A series of huge sea waves caused by shock waves from an earthquake or volcano. Often wrongly called "tidal waves" in English.

Typhoon A violent storm in the Far East. It is called a hurricane when it occurs in the Atlantic Ocean and a cyclone when it occurs in the Indian Ocean.

INDEX

Africa 29, 32
alligators 15, 28
America 9, 10, 31
Antarctic/Arctic 11, 34
Arthur, King 25
Australia 29, 43

barracudas 30
beavers 32
Bermuda Triangle 45

candirus 30
Christianity 43
clams, giant 14
coelacanths 27, 44
crabs 45
crittercams 44
crocodiles 5, 6, 15, 28–29, 31, 33, 43
crustacea 16

Davy Jones' locker 38
deep sea fish 18
dinosaurs 27, 47
dolphins 10, 40–41, 43
dugongs 7, 22

eels 8, 21
electric fish 21, 47
Elizabeth I, Queen of England 11
Europa, Jupiter's moon 45
extinction 9

frogs 33

gods and goddess 7, 24, 33, 36, 38, 41, 42–43

hippopotamuses 32–33, 46

icebergs 34–35
ink 14
islands
  Gilbert 42
  Mariana 12
  Polynesian 43
  Solomon 42

jellyfish 37
Jonah 9

krill 8

lobsters 16

manta rays, "devilfish" 37
Medusa 7
merfolk 6, 22–23, 25, 36, 37, 47
monsters 18–19
  Behemoth 33
  kraken 16, 47
  lake 27
  leviathan 17
  Loch Ness 5, 26–27, 44
  "mowgwyr" 19, 47
  Mokele-Mbembe 33
movies 6
  Anaconda 31
  Clash of the Titans 7
  Crocodile Dundee 29
  Excalibur 25
  Flipper 40
  Free Willy 11
  Godzilla 45
  Hook 29
  James Bond 15
  Jaws 6, 13
  Jungle Book, The 31
  Little Mermaid, The 23
  Moby Dick 9
  Piranha 31
  Splash 23
  Twenty Thousand Leagues Under the Sea 17
myths 7, 16, 21, 22, 23, 24–25, 27, 32, 33, 36, 37, 39, 41, 43

narwhals 11
Noah 37, 39
north west passage 34

oarfish 21
octopuses 14–15, 17
  blue-ringed 14, 46
  giant 14
Odysseus 24–25
orcas (killer whales) 5, 10–11, 40–41, 47
overfishing 9

Pacific 12, 34, 36, 42, 43
Patagonia, Argentina 10
Perseus 7
Peter Pan 29
pikes 30

piranhas 5, 7, 15, 30, 46
pollution 9, 44
Ponting, Herbert 10, 11
Puffer Fish 46

St. Columba 26
St. Paul 38
scientists 11, 37, 39, 44
sea captains 9, 16, 20, 22, 29, 34
seahorses 38, 41
seals 10, 25
sea monks 36
sharks 6, 12–13, 15, 19, 30, 42–43, 47
  basking 13
  blue 42
  bull 46
  goblin 18
  gray reef 13, 42
  great white 13, 46
  hammerhead 12, 18, 42
  "megamouth" 19
  tiger 12
  worship 42–43
shells 14, 41
sirens 6, 24–25
skates 21, 37
snakes 5, 7, 20, 31
  anaconda 31
  cottonmouth 31
  python 15, 31
  sea snakes 20
squids 16–17, 44
stone fish 46
storms 6, 36, 37, 38–39

tentacles 15, 16, 17, 47
Titanic, SS 34
toads 33
tsunami ("tidal waves") 36–37, 47

unicorns 11

venom 31, 33, 37
Vikings 8, 9, 11, 24

walruses 11, 22
whales 5, 7, 8–9, 10–11, 40, 47
  beaked 18–19
  Moby Dick 9
  sperm 9, 16, 44
whirlpools 6, 35